WE COULD ALL BE PERFECT

by Hannah Morley

SAMUEL FRENCH

ISBN 978-0-573-00039-3

concordtheatricals.co.uk
concordtheatricals.com

FOR AMATEUR PRODUCTION ENQUIRIES

United Kingdom and World
excluding North America
licensing@concordtheatricals.co.uk
020-7054-7298

Each title is subject to availability from Concord Theatricals, depending upon country of performance.

This work is published by Samuel French, an imprint of Concord Theatricals Ltd.

USE OF COPYRIGHTED MUSIC

A licence issued by Concord Theatricals to perform this play does not include permission to use the incidental music specified in this publication. In the United Kingdom: Where the place of performance is already licensed by the PERFORMING RIGHT SOCIETY (PRS) a return of the music used must be made to them. If the place of performance is not so licensed then application should be made to PRS for Music (www.prsformusic.com). A separate and additional licence from PHONOGRAPHIC PERFORMANCE LTD (www.ppluk.com) may be needed whenever commercial recordings are used. Outside the United Kingdom: Please contact the appropriate music licensing authority in your territory for the rights to any incidental music.

USE OF COPYRIGHTED THIRD-PARTY MATERIALS

Licensees are solely responsible for obtaining formal written permission from copyright owners to use copyrighted third-party materials (e.g., artworks, logos) in the performance of this play and are strongly cautioned to do so. If no such permission is obtained by the licensee, then the licensee must use only original materials that the licensee owns and controls. Licensees are solely responsible and liable for clearances of all third-party copyrighted materials, and shall indemnify the copyright owners of the play(s) and their licensing agent, Concord Theatricals Ltd., against any costs, expenses, losses and liabilities arising from the use of such copyrighted third-party materials by licensees.

IMPORTANT BILLING AND CREDIT REQUIREMENTS

If you have obtained performance rights to this title, please refer to your licensing agreement for important billing and credit requirements.

WE COULD ALL BE PERFECT was first produced by the Sheffield Theatres in Sheffield, UK on 23rd September 2023. The performance was directed by Ruby Clarke and assistant directed by Rebecca Solomon, with sets by Rūta Irbīte, lighting design by Jessie Addinall, and sound design by Annie May Fletcher. The Casting Director was NadineRennie. The cast was as follows:

A .... Anshula Bain
B .... Heather Forster
C .... Rosa Hesmondhalgh
D .... Alice Walker
E .... Jada-Li Warrican

ABOUT SHEFFIELD THEATRES

SHEFF!ELD
THEATRES

Sheffield Theatres is home to three theatres: the Crucible, the Sheffield landmark with a world-famous reputation; the Playhouse, an intimate, versatile space for getting closer to the action; and the gleaming Lyceum, the beautiful proscenium that hosts the best of the UK's touring shows.

Having held the title 'Regional Theatre of the Year' on four separate occasions, Sheffield Theatres is the ticket to big names and local heroes, timeless treasures and new voices. Committed to investing in the creative leaders of the future, Sheffield Theatres' dedicated talent development hub, The Bank, supports a new cohort of emerging theatre-makers every year.

Sheffield Theatres has a reputation for bold new work. Starting life in the Crucible in 2019, the award winning *Life of Pi* transferred to the West End in 2021 and to Broadway in 2023. This success follows hit musical *Everybody's Talking About Jamie* which also transferred to the West End, toured the UK and enjoyed a feature film release internationally on Amazon Prime in 2021. Both *Life of Pi* and *Everybody's Talking About Jamie* return home to Sheffield Theatres as part of their 2023 – 24 UK and Ireland tours. Last year, *ROCK / PAPER / SCISSORS* was staged across all three theatres to celebrate the 50th anniversary of the Crucible and Playhouse, winning Best Directors at the UK Theatre Awards 2022. Also during the anniversary year, the acclaimed *Accidental Death of an Anarchist* opened the newly named Tanya Moiseiwitsch Playhouse in September 2022. The show transferred to the West End in June 2023. Most recently, Sheffield Theatres, in co-production with the National Theatre and Various Productions, revived *Standing at the Sky's Edge*, returning the show to the Crucible before transferring to the Olivier Theatre and winning two Olivier awards including Best New Musical. The show transfers to the West End in February 2024.

Crucible Lyceum Playhouse 55 Norfolk Street, Sheffield, S1 1DA
sheffieldtheatres.co.uk

CAST AND CREATIVE BIOS

CAST AND CREATIVE BIOS

CHARACTERS

A
B
C
D
E

AUTHOR'S NOTES

Notes On the Text

" / " indicates the point where dialogue overlaps.

Blank space between dialogue indicates a pause. The bigger the blank space, the longer the pause.

In THE PERFECTIONISTS, a line across the page indicates a jump forward in time

It doesn't all happen here. It doesn't all happen now.
Scenes marked "Now" can take place any time between the arrival of smartphones and the present day.
Scenes marked "Before now" can take place any time between the beginning of humanity and then.
"Soon" does what it says on the tin.

Not all of the characters are teenage girls, but everyone can be played by one. There is at least one teenage girl in every scene.
If your cast includes more than five teenage girls, they should all be onstage and involved in THE PERFECTIONISTS.
GIRL is a trans narrative. It should be cast appropriately or cut.

Everyone is feeling everything very strongly at all times, even if they don't want us to know. This is the superpower. The girls are at times deeply weird, deeply obnoxious, deeply ridiculous, and should be taken deeply seriously.

When in doubt with dialogue, try it faster.
Turn up the volume.

FOREWARD

So, I've been thinking about teenage girls for a while (there's literally no way to write that without sounding creepy, sorry) and I have this theory... I reckon if you took everything it is to be a person in the world and boiled it down to its most concentrated form, it would look somthing like a fourteen-year-old girl. The teen girls I've encountered in my life are some of the most kind, cruel, funny, ridiculous, self-conscious, self-loathing, vain, vulnerable, sex-obsessed, brave, terrifying, awful, wonderful people I've met. Always trying, always caring, often despite themselves.

Humanity undiluted.

Maybe this is one reason why, as a society, we don't seem to like them much. They mirror back to us everything we'd see if we cut ourselves open and looked inside, in all its weird, raw discomfort. Or maybe I only think that because I used to be one.

This play came about when two thoughts collided. The first, is that I think one experience perhaps unique to teenage girls is the sudden awareness of being looked at. One moment you're walking down the road in your school uniform shovelling wine gums down your throat undisturbed, the next you realise you're being watched from cars. You can feel eyes on you. It's a surreal experience and nobody really tells you it's going to happen. It's enough to make you paranoid. It certainly makes you self-conscious. The second thought was a curiosity about the link between teenage girls and revolutions. Scroll through TikTok, open any history book, and wherever you find a revolution there's usually a teen girl visible near the centre of it.

The girls in this play are revolutionaries, big and small, but they're also artists. They create, define and improve. They work on perfecting themselves and the world. They find flaws and then strive for better. With this in mind, here are a couple of thoughts that I hope might be helpful in staging this play:

There are lots of moments of looking in the following scenes. Girls being looked at, looking at themselves, at each other and the world. Some of these might be more significant than they first appear. Similarly, each scene contains a revolution, but they might not all be the size you expect. The play deals in micro and macro. At one point in development, we separated the scenes into "violence", "lols", and "violence and lols". I reckon you can turn up the dial on both.

Writing this play, at first, was a bit of a nightmare. An overwhelmingly big thing in a small container. I tried to wrangle it, to tame it, to impose a more logical structure. I tried to confine it to one time period or place, to make it less weird, to make it easier to understand. I wanted its politics to be more realistic, to explain that it's not about men but power, or violence. I tried to fit every teen experience inside it; the scenes spilled over at the sides. What Ruby, Grace and I discovered during redrafting is that it probably helps to approach this play feeling first, rather than thinking.

The play is a bit of a teenage girl and, at first, I tried to dilute it. We learnt it's much better when you don't.

HM x

ACKNOWLEDGEMENTS

My catchphrase during rehearsals was "I just can't get over how many people there are". I blurted it mid-conversation, voice-noted it to friends, I honestly got bored of hearing myself say it. There are so many people to thank for getting this play on the stage and this book in your hands. Here are the names of just some of them:

Thanks to Ruby Clarke, first and foremost. You talk about this play in a way that makes me want to follow you into battle – which, as a fainter who doesn't like conflict or being told what to do, is saying a lot. None of this would have happened without your passion, skill and perseverance. And to Grace Gummer, for your script wizardry and for inventing the fizzy fortnight. You got me across the finish line. Thank you.

Thank you to Robert Hastie and everyone at Sheffield Theatres. This theatre is where I first saw new writing as a teen. I'll forever be grateful that you lent me the stage for a while.

To Alice, Anshula, Heather, Jada-Li, Rosa, and the entire production team for your creativity and generosity in rehearsals. And to the actors who lent their talent and experience during R&D. I want to be all of you when I grow up.

To Grace Stone and Hippolyte Poirier for performing an early version of Send Nudes and not mentioning my bad directing; an act of diplomacy that's extremely out of character for at least one of you. And thanks for everything else too. To Dan Ireson, Neil McPherson, Melissa Dunne, Tommo Fowler for their early belief. To everyone at Concord Theatricals, the Finborough, Radius, BBC Writersroom, and the Channel 4 Playwrights Prize for their support. To Matt Hartley, Amy Rosenthal, and all at Arvon; the first scenes for this were written at Totleigh. To Debbie and Paul Mellors for leading me to acting. And to Mr Foster. Because back in Year 6 I said I would.

Most of all...Mum, Dad, Tom, and all my family. I love you. Thank you. Sorry the play is so weird. And to my friends. God knows how I got so lucky. If I could show thirteen-year-old me anything from the future, it would be you.

This is a play for teenage girls.

1

Secret – Now

(Darkness.)

*(**A**'s face lit up by a screen. Hiding under her bed, recording herself on a phone. The camera is pointing directly up her nose at a deeply unflattering angle. Uncoordinated and unselfconscious.)*

(She breathes heavily like a psychopath.)

(Then –.)

A. Hellooooo

can you see me?

what if it's what if it's what if it's this. what if it's that actually I'm completely fully invisible. like maybe it could be that
and this isn't even
like it's actually that

my best things are werewolves the colour turquoise dairylea lunchables God and the new boy in the flat downstairs I like hissss hair and also the way he moves his hands he's probably definitely the actual love of my life and we will be mermaids but I'm also going to be prime minister and president and do science my worst things are broccoli, fractions and war

sex

s

sex

bugger

I think I'm probably literally incredible

fuck

I'm sorry God.

Fuck.

(**A** *slaps a hand over her mouth to stifle a laugh.)*

I'm not even supposed to have this

First Love – Before Now

(**A** *squats.* **B** *stands.*)

A. I want to know everything about you

B. Spend all of your day with me

A. I want to know even things you don't know about yourself

B. every day all day for at least one whole year

A. Let's make a pact that we don't spend any time with anyone else

B. BLOOD PACT

A. YESSS

B. no other ladies or other maids or or or

A. never

B. we don't dilute this with other friends

A. other friends take you away from me

B. Ask if I can ask if I can ask if I can move up to your room in the big house

A. I'm going to move down to the servants' quarters and sleep in your bed and wear one sad woollen outfit and eat things that are exclusively brown

B. or that

A. maybe I'll contract a disease, it'll be *amazing*

B. let's spend the rest of our lives together

A. forever. Both wear pink

B. brothers for husbands

A. children who marry each other

B. I want to stay within five paces of you at all times

A. yes

B. at all times

A. Yes

B. no but At All Times

A. I want to literally open you up and scoop out your organs and climb inside your skin so we can become one person

B. okay yes no yes okay

A. Sorry is that too much? It's just I feel like we are actually already one person think/ing the same thoughts... constantly...all...the time

B. ing the s...same thoughts...consistently alwa...of the time.
Wow!

A. Yeah
Maybe we were twins

B. !!!

A. Non-identical twins separated at birth and taken to different parts of the

B. dropped in a basket in the river or adopted or

A. and I ended up massively rich

B. Yeah

A. and you ended up

B. yeah poor yeah

A. Okay on the three on the three okay say your birthday. One two three / *February the twelfth*

B. *The first of June*
But still

A. I'm going to eat you

B. I'm going to eat you

A. Not if I eat you first.

B. I think we are literally exactly the same.

A. I feel like I've had you forever. Like my foot or my spleen or

B. I feel completely the same

(**A** *holds out a hand.)*

(**B** *takes it and pulls her up from the chamber pot.)*

A. What's your name?

Refusal – Before Now

(**B** *lies face down.)*

A. Get up.

B. Mmph

A. Get up.

B. Mmph

A. Just get up and do something.

B. I can't

A. Get up
Get up
Get up
Get up

(**B** *screams into a pillow.)*

Can you get up now please?

Get up
Come on. We have to get going

Sunglasses – Now

(**A** *might be wearing a swimming costume.*)

A. how do you know though?

B. It's just how it is.

A. why is it like that though?

B. because it keeps everything, it's just the way things are, it keeps everything safe. You put your money in a safe place, in a bank, and they look after it for you and it grows when it's there too so you get more over time. Like a like a mushroom in the dark. or a person I suppose

A. or a sea-monkey

B. or a probably and then when you need the money you can just take it from the

A. but who owns it?

B. you do

A. but you don't have it. They have it

B. you own it they're just looking after it for you. you couldn't have it yourself could you because then everything would be

A. why can't

B. everything would be chaos wouldn't it

A. how do you own something if you don't have it

B. because. well because everyone's agreed. you just do.

A. but

B. it's just how it's always been done

A. that's a stupid reason to do anything

B. er!

A. that's a silly reason to do anything. why doesn't

B. You'll understand when you're older

A. what if

B. It works. it's just a system that

A. but what if they don't give it back

B. works. they wouldn't do that

A. but what if they didn't though

B. they have to give it back

A. but what if they didn't

B. they always do

A. okay but what if they didn't

B. look at that dog

A. You don't know do you

B. Yes I do

A. explain then

B. well I don't want to now

A. but

B. I could

A. why's he looking at me?

B. who?

There's nobody looking at you.

A. that man over there in the sunglasses

B. there's nobody
where?

There isn't anybody looking at you.

A. there

There

B. that sun's hot isn't it?

*(**A** waves at the man.)*

A. can I have an ice cream now?

Gramophone – Before Now

(Five girls and a gramophone.)

A. Shh shhhh

B. quickly

C. watch the door watch the

D. I'm watching

E. we shouldn't

B. who has it?

E. really we shouldn't

C. ow!

B. do you have it?

C. owwwwuh

A. sh!

E. uncle says it is the devil's sounds

C. she trod on my foot!

A. SHH!

E. and if

B. oh

C. you shh!

B. oh I have it

E. and if we listen uncle says there is a darkness that will climb inside our bodies and take control and wake us in the night and make us experience confusing

A. ready?

E. confusing sensations

D. They're in the drawing room

(They gather round the gramophone.)

*(**B** places the record on the turntable.)*

E. wait

*(**A** drops the needle and it cranks into action.)*

(Four notes of a Rachmaninoff symphony and then the girls completely lose their fucking minds.)

A. !!!!/!!!!!!!

B. OH MY / GOD

C. OH MY / OH MY

D. OH / GOD OH MY

E. Oh oh oh oh oh

*(**A** pulls the needle away.)*

A. !!!!!!!!!!!!!!!!!!!!!

B. STOP. I DON'T. I

C. ***WHAT?!!?***

A. shhh FUCK shhh

C. THIS IS / THE BEST THING THAT HAS EVER BEEN WRITTEN THIS IS

D. no but wait wait wait / wait wait wait wait wait wait

E. oh / oh oh oh

C. I CANNOT BREATHE

B. shhhh shhh play some more play some

(**A** *drops the needle.*)

(The music resumes.)

(Everyone silently loses their shit.)

A. !!

B. !!!!!!!!!!!!!!!!!!!!!!!!!!!!!!!!!?!?!?!?

C. !!! !!!!!!!!! !!!!!!!!!!!!!!!!!!!!

D. ?????!!!!!!!!!!!!!!!!!!!!!!

E. 😮

(**A** *lifts the needle.*)

B. SHIT

C. wait can I just say the Strings though

A. wait can I just say the bit where is Rises

B. okay wait can I just say the Tone though

D. wait

C. can I just say the doo / duh duh dooooo

A. duh / duh doooooow

B. YES deeeee oh my god

D. wait can I just. can / I just

B. I'm crying. Look. I'm crying

A. SHE'S CRYING

B. There is water coming out of my eyes

C. I cried

A. I think I cried too

D. I'm welling. I'm definitely welling

B. look

C. doo duh duh doooooh

E. I can't believe that's a thing that exists

C. go back to the beginning I want you to hear the

(They cling on to each other.)

Pedalo – Now

A. Tell me what you like about me

B. Is this a game?

A. like what are the things

B. the

A. specifically

B. Right. I'm just trying to make sure that the water doesn't get in the

A. tell me. please. you don't have to be looking

B. I'm not going to be looking

A. okay

B. I'm not going to be looking I'm going to be navigating us back to shore

A. that's fine

B. What is this?

A. just say first. please

B. why are we doing this?

okay

okay

I suppose

I suppose I like that you're funny

I like that you just say things. like this. this is a thing you've just said out of nowhere and it's, I don't really know what's happening to be honest

erm
you're weirdly good at fractions actually. that's something I've noticed
you're kind
you have a good personality. I think you're quite nice overall and /patient

A. what else?

B. or maybe not

A. is that it?

B. well it's quite hard to think and pedal

you're actually really quite weird generally speaking like generally quite odd and I appreciate that
and I suppose you try hard

A. no

B. you always try hard I think / you're always trying

A. I don't. that's not true

B. I like that. and you care a lot

A. what else?

B. you're clever

no?

A. what about my

B. your what?

you make a good cup of tea

A. Do you want me?

B. what?

why would you ask that?
why

A. Do you?

B. why are you asking me that?

A. I think you might

what could I make you do?

B. stop that

A. do you?

B. stop.
what do you want me to say?
what do you actually want me to say to that?

A. I don't know

B. you have abnormally neat handwriting

A. Is that it? that's everything?

B. I love you

A. that isn't one. but thanks

Supermarket One – Now

(The girl from **SECRET**. *Bundled up in warm layers and carrying a large backpack. On the move and trying to stay hidden.)*

(She spots something in the distance. Stops.)

(Takes her phone out and starts filming, until –.)

(A sudden noise startles her and she runs.)

2

Dance – Before Now

*(**B** and **C** are dancing.)*

A. Teach me.

B. Get away.

A. Will you teach me that?

B. get away get away

A. I want to learn. It's beautiful.

B. No. It's too many. No space. They will see.

A. Are you not allowed?

Is she not allowed?

B. Shoo!

Hss!

A. This foot then this arm here. This. This.

*(**A** stumbles.)*

C. Hooo! She is bad.

*(**A** tries again.)*

B. Not like that.

A. Show me.

B. Too young.

A. Am not. Show me. Teach me.

C. Do it. If they come, we can tell them we were dancing.

B. Dancing ha

A. Aren't you?

C. Ha

B. Fighting.

C. Dancing ha

A. It looks the same.
What's the difference?

(**C** *alters the dance to slap* **A** *playfully.)*

C. People in our way.

Thirst Trap – Now

(As fast you can.)

A. First

B. First

C. First!

D. First

E. First

B. First / comment

A. omg first

C. First comment!

E. /First!

D. First!

C. Look! at! him!

B. heart eyes heart eyes heart / eyes

A. Yaaaaaaaaa/aaaaaaaaaaaaaaaaaaaaaaaaaaaaaaaaaaaa aaaaaaaas!

E. I love you I love you so much

D. crying face

E. look at him tho

C. this photo cleared my skin

B. COME TO BRAZIL

A. I can't even

D. ahoy there

E. flames!

C. this photo got me pergnamt

B. flamesflamesflamesflames

A. cat

E. fire. heart. palm tree

A. First comment!

B. screaming

D. holyshit

A. adore u

C. *this photo got my pregmamt

E. you look sooo good!!! he looks soooooooo good

B. COME TO BRAZIL

A. Gross

D. Follow back!

C. I Died

A. Dead

E. deceased

B. rip me

D. follow me back!

E. excuse me?? sir??? sir

D. **ARMS**

A. stop it

D. **LOOK AT HIS ARMS**

E. red sweating face red sweating face red sweating face

C. *prugnant

B. HELP

D. I need 2 lie down

C. everyone be normal!

A. I AM A SEAGULL AND THIS MAN IS CHIPS

E. I cannot breathe!

D. babygirl

B. ice cream

C. JUST PUSH ME IN A LAKE ALREADY

E. I have lost all access to oxygen!!!!

A. puking face

B. ice cream ice cream

D. screaming

E. yelling

C. crying face

A. dying. I'm dying

B. I

D. screaming

C. crying

A. throwing up

C. CATAPULT ME INTO THE SUN

E. hi sweetie this is linda your mom's friend? we lived next door on Cleveland Road?

B. 2 month and I will see you

D. Make money online without having to leave your home

A. COME TO LEEDS

B. COME TO BRAZIIIIIIIL

E. the blue house on Cleveland road. we had a dalmatian

C. JUST TOSS ME INTO THE OCEAN I CANT

B. I have stage four cancer and seeing you makes my day so much better

D. I LOVE YOU

C. u r hot and I am s u f f e r i n g

E. Second!

B. tongue tongue water droplets

A. tongue water droplets aubergine

C. DROPKICK ME INTO A VOLCANO

D. my dog d worded today sad face

E. dm me for hot spicyxxxxx pics

A. FUCK

B. COME TO BRAZIL

E. I love you more than anything

A. ambulance

C. omg step on me

D. the state of these comments

B. tHe StAtE oF tHeSe CoMmEnTs

A. please read this and please do not ignore. the government they are killing girls in my country

E. red heart

B. run me over with your car!

D. Is everyone in these comments a fucking teenage g–

C. Second!

A. children. they are killing

E. ur so babygirl

D. Really respect your work, man

B. Just choke me already. god

C. *pergmont

E. sweetie this is linda again you should put a shirt on you look cold

A. they take away our voi–

C. I adore u

D. unalive yourself

B. help me

E. woahhhh daddy

C. I would let you chop my arms off

A. No one can have you

B. Punch me in the face

D. please

E. first!

C. second!

D. Cat!

A. Punch me right in the fucking face

Self-Conscious – Now

A. Just put your coat on. Honestly nobody gives a shit what you look like. Nobody's looking at you.

B. yes they are. everybody is

A. Oh for God's sake

B. they weren't before but they are now. everyone's looking at me

First Day – Before Now

*(**B** stares into water.)*

A. Come and play.

B. I can't see it.

A. You'll turn into a daffodil.

B. Can you see it?

A. You look the same. You always do

B. There must have been a moment.

A. One. Two. Three. Catch!

Fucksake

B. Come and look.

A. Then play.

B. What do you see?

A. Fen creatures ready to suck you in. Feed on children from your township. They're all absolutely going to eat you.

B. Am I pretty?

A. What's the game?

B. Just say.
If I'm ugly you can tell me. I never thought of it before.

A. Hmm.

*(She holds **B**'s face in her hands. Squishes it.)*

Can't tell.

B. I just see my face. Is it a good one? I always had it with me. See it here every day and I can't catch it changing.

A. I can hold my breath literally forever. Watch.

*(***A*** sticks her head in the water for quite a long time.)*

B. my mouth is definitely bigger

Soldiers One – Now

*(***A*** sets up her phone and performs a dance routine. TikTok-style. It's a little stumbling and self-conscious.)*

(Perhaps something familiar like "Made You Look" by Meghan Trainor.[*]*)*

(You can tell she's watching herself.)

---

* A licence to produce *We Could All Be Perfect* does not include a performance licence for "Made You Look". The publisher and author suggest that the licensee contact PRS to ascertain the music publisher and contact such music publisher to license or acquire permission for performance of the song. If a licence or permission is unattainable for "Made You Look", the licensee may not use the song in *We Could All Be Perfect* but should create an original composition in a similar style or use a similar song in the public domain. For further information, please see the Music and Third-Party Materials Use Note on page iii.

Supermarket Two – Now

(**MAN** *has a gun.*)

SECRET. oh my. oh my oh my god

MAN. Where have you come from?

SECRET. oh my god

MAN. Did someone tell you I'm here? Did someone

SECRET. you're the first person I've seen in days you

MAN. Did someone send you?

SECRET. oh my god

MAN. Stay back.

SECRET. I just it's not I no I just

MAN. Get the fuck back!

SECRET. okay
okay

Sir
can you put that down please?
nobody sent me, I promise. I was just walking up from downtown and I saw the sign with the lights on. supermarket. Ha! They're still on, did you know? I can't actually remember the last time I saw lights on

MAN. Where did you see people?
Were they close?

SECRET. yeah. or not close but. there was a soldier in the park a few days ago. I shouted but he didn't hear me

MAN. You shouldn't do that

SECRET. wait, you're living in the supermarket?
Is there still food in there?

MAN. back

SECRET. do you have food in there?
are there more people?
do you have power?

MAN. How old are you?

SECRET. you know there's fighting downtown?

MAN. You shouldn't go downtown

SECRET. can I come inside? you have food right?

MAN. We're full

SECRET. I'm hungry. please. I'm so hungry

MAN. There's no room

SECRET. How many of you are there?

MAN. We're full

3

Proposal – Before Now

A. and?

B. He has allowed it.

A. Oh! Oh!

B. Truly

A. I am so happy

B. And I. So happy

A. Truly

B. Shall I?

(**A** *nods.* **B** *kneels.*)

My dearest. Radiant beauty and fine young lady. I have spoken with your father and he says that we're we're we're good to go, as it were, so would you do me the honour
nay the privilege
of finally
finally
becoming my Wife?

A. No.

B. um

A. Sorry. I'm so sorry. I didn't mean to say that.

I'm not sure what came over me

B. that's

A. a a a turn or

B. okay

A. the heat probably

B. right yes

A. Could you try that again?

I think I just need to get in the mood.

B. Will you marry me?

A. No.

B. Really?!

A. I don't mean to say it, it just keeps coming out. Just keep

B. Will you marry

A. Nope

B. perhaps

A. No

B. could

A. Nuh-uh

B. would you consi

A. Nooo

B. will y

A. No. Nope. Absofuckinglutely n–

(**A** *slaps a hand over her mouth.)*

B. Should I–?

(**B** *goes to stand, but then –.)*

A. Do you think you could hate me a little bit first?

B. Pardon?

A. Just a little. I think it would help.

B. What are you doing?

A. It's just. I'd quite like for you to be completely repulsed by me initially. Do you think we could start again and try that?

B. the proposal or?

A. The whole thing. You might think I'm uncouth or wild or a bit dirty perhaps. Entirely caught up in my own brain. Yes, if you could find me entirely disagreeable that would be great

B. right?

A. If you could be physically angered but the sight of me. And I'm working something out here perhaps then very slowly through a series of chance encounters I don't know perhaps we weeeee are forced to make terse conversation while my sister dances with your friend or. ooh! perhaps I could tutor your young ward who's actually the same age as me and you realise that I am clever which is very confusing to you

B. I don't have a ward

A. but but but hot

B. crikey. right. um

A. Or there's a blizzard!

B. a blizzard

A. And we become stranded in a hostile climate, forced to take shelter in an abandoned hut by a frozen lake with only our bodies for warmth and there's just one single bed and you offer to sleep on the cold floorboards like a dalmatian because you are a gentleman and I tell you not to be so repressed and just get in the fucking bed with me and I take you

B. oh

A. just take you right there just. consume each other and. just this grasping crawling. or maybe you flee to a different country to escape the sheer force of how much you love me. just like this ache of I shouldn't I shouldn't want her but I do. her Personality it's just. I want the force of how much you want me to completely wipe out how much you hate me. I want you to hate how much you love me. For you to wake up in the night screaming in awe at my existence I want it to feel biblical to you. It has teeth and jaws and hot breath and you want to climb inside. I want to clasp your face between my hands and lick it all over just lick you and for you to want it. I'm going to eat you alive and you're going to say thank you. Nothing gentle. I want you grasping for me in the darkness

B. yes

A. I want you to want me without your consent

B. Yes

A. I want you to propose to me like it's the worst day of your life and I want you sobbing with fucking gratitude when I say yes

B. Yes

A. Then I might feel like I had a little say in the matter.

Lessons – Now

(Five girls film themselves. They all have ring lights. **B** *applies makeup expertly.* **C** *applies it with creativity and joy but zero skill.* **D** *is bare-faced and crying.)*

(More and more makeup is added through the scene.)

(Let them talk over each other as much as possible.)

A. Hi /guys!

B. hi /guys

C. hi /everyone!

B. get ready with / me

A. get ready with me to. oh oops

B. okay so I'm in a massive rush cos I was supposed to be at a party like an hour ago but... / get ready with me to sneak out of my parent's house

C. I'm whispering because this is my older sister's makeup box. she doesn't exactly one hundred / percent know that I have it

B. storytime!

C. get ready /with me

A. this is um I just thought I'd make a video about this because I've been thinking about like confidence a lot. and just being like. better. / these are my tips on how to be your like your best self

B. so technically I might be kind of grounded right now but at this / party there's this boy

A. and there's this girl

B. obviously

A. in my class

D. hi guys um

A. and she is so / perfect

C. I should probably actually say that I don't really wear makeup on a like a day to / day bas—

A. like I really like her. / um

C. keepin it oh natural. but yeah I thought I'd show you what I do when I want to look a bit more. makeupy. / okay so

A. and I just want her to see but I guess she / thinks I'm shy

D. this is a really difficult /one for me

B. I'm gonna teach you how to do my perfect sexy no make-up-make-up-your-lips-but-better

C. just like spread it / all around

A. and I'm completely /not

B. you're welcome!

A. so tip number one. this is gonna sound stupid this is silly but. like. pretend that you're famous / like when you walk in a room

B. your liner needs to be sharp. like knife / sharp seriously

C. it's really important to have a really shiny face

D. I know that I've let you all down. that I need to do better to be better./ I feel horrible. I'm so ashamed

A. everyone's looking at you. but in a good way. I kind of have this idea that if you're famous then everyone wants to be you

B. isn't that amazing?

A. and then maybe you want to be you too

C. that actually. that looks really good

(It doesn't.)

B. oh my /god

D. I could tell you this girl made my life hell for literal /years

C. It's just paint /basically

D. that this girl was abusive to me and to others. but I'm not here to make excuses.

A. um

D. All I can say is I'm sorry

E. Hi guys!

B. I look amazing!

E. get ready with me

D. I am not normally a violent / person

A. I'll tell you tip two tomorrow. keep / watching!

D. please keep watching.

E. take your curler and then with your other hand

D. I feel like if you stop, I might not exist.

E. you're going to pick up your phone and google this name, okay?

(The lights flicker.)

this is important

(The lights flicker.)

this girl was taken from the street on her way home by her country's police just for wearing

Muse – Before Now

(**A** *is painting* **B**.)

A. Left.

Left.

Left.

Left Stop.

Up.
Up.
Go *up*.

No not like that with your

B. WITH MY

A. Yes with your

Up up down up STOP

Good.

What are you doing?

B. WHAT?

A. Why are you doing that with your

B. WHAT?

A. Take the hel **Take the / helmet off**

B. I'M GOING TO TAKE THE HELMET OFF

A. What are you doing with your face?

B. Looking at you

A. No. Before, what were you

B. When?

A. Your your your mouth

B. My

A. There. That.

B. Smiling? I'm smiling. I was smiling.

A. Why?

B. I'm having an alright time.

A. What?

B. I've been told I have a good smile.

A. You're not you. She wouldn't have been smiling.

B. She might have been smiling.

A. Put your hand

B. She was big into God wasn't she?

A. Will you put your hand

B. Her whole thing was that she was big into God and so yeah she's dying but she's also going to see him soon in the

A. Up. Left.

B. And to be near and maybe to touch and there'll be no more war which yeah she was also into but seems like a lot of of of effort and I'm not sure she was even having the best time actually. And this hand she's reaching out

A. In fear

B. No towards

(**B** *puts down his paintbrush.)*

A. In distress she's a

B. reaching up towards

A. a martyr. She's about to be burnt alive. Her physical body is going to be set on fire. Stay still. The metal of her armour is about to melt and stick to her flesh which is about to peel and bubble and her bones will turn black and her eyeballs will boil in her head and everyone is going to watch and so I highly doubt that she would be smiling.

She would be Sad.

B. Sad.

You don't think that she'd be sc

A. Up.

B. I said you don't think that she'd be screa

Fans – Before Now

(Everyone is screaming at all times. There might be more than three girls.)

A. WHO ARE WE SCREAMING FOR?!

B. WHAT?!

A. **WHY ARE WE SCREAMING?!**

B. ONE SECOND!

(To **C.***)* **WHY ARE WE SCREAMING?**

C. WHAT?!?!

A. ***WHY. ARE. WE. SCREAMING?!?!?***

C. I DON'T KNOW!

(They're still screaming.)

A. IT FEELS GOOD!

Pregnant – Now or Before Now

*(**A** tries to hold a door closed. Heavily pregnant. Sobbing.)*

*(**B** tries to push it open.)*

B. what have you done?
what have you done?
what have you done?
what have you done?
what have you

Supermarket Three – Now

(The second girl is **B** *from* **LESSONS***.)*

SECRET. There's a person living inside the supermarket. I spoke to him the first day I got here

LESSONS. I followed the lights on the sign

SECRET. Me too

LESSONS. I only came out to find food

SECRET. he has everything in there. there are bins out the back and he throws rubbish out sometimes. tins with stuff left in the bottom that he hasn't eaten. I got a whole packet of ice cream cones once

LESSONS. woah really?

SECRET. just the wafer bits and they'd gone a bit soft but I think the freezers in there are still working.

LESSONS. I can't believe you're here. I can't actually believe there's anyone else here

SECRET. I know. hi!

LESSONS. hi!

SECRET. this is so weird!
bleugh

LESSONS. bleugh weird bleugh

aren't you freezing?

SECRET. kind of. you forget though

LESSONS. how are you actually still alive?

SECRET. there's an old travel agent across the road that's a good place for sleeping. some of the roof is gone but there's a store cupboard you can get in if you make yourself small. we could take turns in that if you wanted? I sleep in the day while it's warmer and then normally I come and sit here to watch the doors from like four, in case he comes out. like he has to come out eventually. it's kind of just a case of

LESSONS. waiting

SECRET. yeah basically

oh. he has a gun too so

do you want to stay?

4

Body – Now

*(**A** is wearing something with **B**'s face on.)*

(She is holding cake.)

A. It's you

B. Oh my god

A. It's you

B. Fucking hell oh my god

A. you're there

B. You made me jump. How did you get in here?

A. you're right there. you're

B. There should've been someone at the door

A. There wasn't. or there was but

B. a security

A. There was but I waited
I waited until he walked away for a second. I don't think it's anything, like I think probably all it is is he's gone off for a phone call or some food or to do a quick wee. and I really wasn't planning on coming in here I just – I saw him go and the sign said dressing rooms and then I thought – what I thought was – sorry "piss"

B. piss?

A. I shouldn't have said that thing before about doing a quick wee. "Piss" would have been better. more – less –

B. you

A. or actually maybe probably not mentioning any kind of uri ur urinatory stu–

Urination.

B. You can't be in here

A. Sorry, I keep forgetting you can see me

B. You need to leave

A. But I brought you this

B. Now

A. But I made it for you.

(She goes to give the cake.)

(He steps back quickly so she can't touch him.)

Don't you want it?

Here

B. Just stay back alright

A. you're frightened

B. How old are you?

A. why are you frightened?

B. if they find you in here

A. It's just lemon

B. lemon

A. the cake

B. ah. yeah. sorry. I'm allergic.

A. No you're not.

B. I am. sorry. can't eat it

A. no

B. sorry?

A. you're not. I'd know that.

B. what?

A. you aren't allergic, I would know. I know everything about you.

(She takes another step towards him.)

B. Okay, have you got a knife?

A. For the cake?

B. or a gun or

A. I. I don't think that would be the best way to

B. what do you want do you want to kidnap me

A. oh my god

B. you're going to say that I did something to you is that

A. no!

B. you want to lock me in a basement

A. no

B. you want to chop me up and put each of my fingers in individual jars/ is that

A. no. that's not I /didn't think

B. You want to wear my skin as clothing

A. No

B. Do you want money? because I can give you money

A. no? no

B. I can give you what you want. Just tell me.

A. sorry, I'm going to leave now because I've accidentally been a complete psychopath

B. No

A. I definitely have

B. Well

A. much obliged kind sir
and anyway he'll be back from his quick w – piss soon so. Unless he's actually doing a number tw– Christ

I think I just wanted to tell you that you mean
That your music is art and it means
I wanted for you to know that I

(**A** *and* **B** *look at each other.*)

I think I just wanted this actually

Twins – Now

B. What does it look like?

A. Don't want to talk about it.

B. Why were you looking anyway?

A. Interested. Haven't you looked?

B. Stuck a finger up there once

A. What did it feel like?

B. Kind of

like
Rural?

A. Huh

B. I'm borrowing this dress

A. Why haven't you looked?

B. Gives me the heebie-jeebies

A. What?

B. well it's just odd isn't it because you've never seen it because it's tucked away down there just you know lying dormant or whatever it makes it into a thing

A. Lying Dormant

B. like a creature in a novel. You never see it so it becomes this terrible thing in your imagination. And it's on you you know it's *on* you and you can't escape it

A. Can't escape your

B. Your hoo-hah yes

A. Mother says we should use the scientific terms

B. Worse. They make it sound malevolent

A. Vagina. / Vulva. Cervix

B. Like a dark lord

A. I'm hungry

B. "We have commands from the mighty Cervix"

A. I'm going to eat something

B. "Destroyer of all"

(**A** *eats something.*)

A. You know what your problem is don't you?

B. My sister is a degenerate whore / who examines her own genitals

A. I've seen yours and you haven't

B. in her spare time. What?

A. I've seen your bits.

B. No you haven't when?

A. Identical twins. So, if I've seen mine then I've seen yours too because surely *everything's* identical

B. but

A. You could have anything down there and you wouldn't know. It could have teeth and little eyes like buttons or maybe it's nothing maybe it's just a smooth mound like a doll or maybe it's something else entirely something without a name or it could be any colour or just like a second mouth or it could be a Bad one you could have a really really Bad one and I know and you don't

B. but then yours would be too

A. At least I know what we're dealing with.

Fork – Now

(**A** *puts a Dictaphone in front of* **B**.)

A. Whenever you're ready.

B. Okay.

Well.

I guess I didn't think about it beforehand. I was just eating my dinner on the bench and I saw it. Just this ginormous arse. In oil and. Just massive. Just absolutely big yeah big big big big. Wide like a cow's. Big. And him stood over her and her arm outstretched like this and then I was stepping over the barrier. Nobody tried to stop me or nothing not Miss or any of the other kids because I don't think anybody ever thought I was the kind of girl to do something like that. But all I could think of was if this girl was me and somebody had painted my arse like that then I would want somebody to do it.

It was of Medusa before the snakes. I learnt this after so I can't even claim that's why

Basically what happened was that first Medusa was just like this teenage priestess kicking around the temple. And the deal was that she was supposed to be a virgin, right? But then Poseidon sees her and he can't help himself so he rapes her in the temple. Just rapes her. No you know not even bothering to pretend to be a swan or anything. Just rapes this girl. And then Athena's pissed at Medusa because she was supposed to be a virgin that was like that was the agreement. Um. And that's why she gives her the snake head and the eyes that will turn a man to stone. And Medusa never turned a woman to stone not one and I would say this is probably why. But Athena's not pissed at Poseidon, she's pissed at Medusa.

Anyway, canvas is actually thicker than you think? I had to kind of stab it first, just stab this fork into this painting of her wide wide arse. And then drag down. And that was unfortunate because the sound of the tearing was actually quite like the sound of a fart and then also all the pesto on my fork just sort of left this green smear like baby shit all over. Like dribbling down her leg. That was. That wasn't what I intended.

But then when they were dragging me away, all I could think about was the violence of it. And how tearing canvas feels like tearing skin. And that I was just as bad, maybe just as bad as him that painted her like that. Because the power that I felt when I tore through her was maybe also the power that he felt when he painted her like that transferred through the metal of the fork to me. Boy, girl whatever. And maybe that power was why he painted her like that because in that moment when I did it there was a kind of joy.

And I would do it again. But I dunno if it's because of the freeing her or because of the joy.

Either way I don't think her arse was that relevant.

There should be a painting of the before, I think. Before the snakes. Before Poseidon. Like.

Medusa was a teenage

Soldiers Two – Now

*(***A***,* **B** *and* **C** *perform a synchronised TikTok-style dance. Cooler, more confident and relaxed.)*

(Perhaps we start to realise the movements are the same as in dance.)

Coup – Now

(**C** *is applying lipstick in a mirror.)*

A. we know something about you?

C. Sorry what?

B. She said we know something.

About you.

C. Erm. Okay.

A. don't you want to know what it is?

C. What what is?

B. Ha. 'what what'

C. What?

B. We saw

A. we saw something and now we know it. so

C. Wait. Who even are you?

A. funny

B. Yeah that's hilarious

C. Are you new?

A. that's

you

you tormented me for upwards of two years. you tripped me over every morning at the gates. you locked me in Mrs Coleridge's big cupboard. you ruined my dalmatian painting. no? you called me pigface. braceface. pizzaface. fuckface? you told everyone that my parents were twins with each other and that's why I look the

way I do but that they actually couldn't help it because they were very much in love. at advent assembly you set my hair a bit on fire with your christingle.
stop. laughing.

B. Sorry

A. *fuck*

B. just some of it's like objectively funny

A. you don't remember any of this?

C. No

A. Nothing?

C. Not really but it does sound pretty consistent with stuff that I would do so sure whatever.

A. Turn back round.

Turn back round and face me.

Tell her

B. Samson Jones.

A. Tell her when.

B. Friday last.

A. Tell her where.

B. Back room of the church hall. Saw you go in. And then him

A. And after that

B. Heard stuff.

C. So?

A. Just interesting is all. Just some information that we have. Just something we found out. And a video that we made.

C. a

A. Just a little video

C. it wasn't

B. Did you like it?

C. You know what. Yeah. Yeah I did.

B. That might be even funnier.

A. So then we did some more finding out, didn't we?

B. I think it's funnier. Are you completely in love with him?

C. I

A. Does anyone know your mum's a prozzie?

B. Sex worker

A. Yeah sorry sex worker

Do they know?

Can you hear me?

Helloooooo?

C. no

A. Thought not.
The absolute state of you. Swanning round like you're I don't know like you're golden and looking down on everybody and actually you're pond scum. It's about being beautiful on the inside and you're about as ugly on the inside as I ever saw.
Are you training in the family business?

C. no

A. Are you going to teach your little sister next?

C. that isn't

B. Are you just a very large amount of a whore?

C. Shut up.

A. Oh I wouldn't. I really really wouldn't.

B. yeah don't

A. Not unless you want us to make a Big Announcement. Do you want that?

Didn't think so.

Okay so here's how it goes. From now on you don't exist. You don't matter. You're not relevant. I look around and I can't find you. Someone will go oh remember that girl the one with the lipstick and the other person they'll think and think and then go no. I don't remember. You are a blank. You are an absence of space. Even your parents will forget you if your dad even knew you existed in the first place which I'm very much starting to doubt. And if you ever, ever think about becoming not a blank, not a nothing. I will come to your grotty little piss house in the middle of the night and put a pillow in your mouth and press and press. I will come and cut off your head. I will shave every bit of that bitch ugly rat hair off your head and sell it to that woman by the river for about 50p. I will erase you. I will delete you from existence.

This is a New World Order.

Do you understand that?

Is that penetrating your thick hea

Supermarket Four – Now

(**SECRET** *is weak but alive.*)

LESSONS. is there a knife

SECRET. this is a travel agent

LESSONS. or a gun or

SECRET. you're not going to do that

LESSONS. I might have to do that

SECRET. you can't

LESSONS. I might have to

SECRET. there's a stapler. is that anything? you could threaten to staple him

LESSONS. he has a gun doesn't he? I could take his gun

SECRET. don't do that

LESSONS. I have to

SECRET. please don't do that

LESSONS. he has food in there. and it's all in tins and if there's power which there must be because of the sign then the freezers will be working and there's enough in there to keep him alive forever. even if there's more people than just him, that's food for a city isn't it? water that hasn't been snow

look at me

you're going to d-word soon

SECRET. no I'm not

LESSONS. you're going to starve. or freeze. and then me too if nothing changes

SECRET. but

LESSONS. it's true

SECRET. we just have to wait

LESSONS. how long are we going to keep waiting

SECRET. can you put more brochures on the fire

LESSONS. he'll be in there forever if we let him

SECRET. Italy camping or old people cruises

LESSONS. Italy. keep old people

if I sneak up where he can't see me. if I close my eyes and just keep hitting

SECRET. there has to be another way

LESSONS. He isn't coming out. He's never coming out. We have to

SECRET. shh
wait
I think I saw the light flic

5

Market – Now

(At least half of the characters in this scene are men. **D** *sends emails on their phone throughout.)*

A. We're very excited

B. that's cool

C. and we appreciate your time we really

A. We do

C. we wouldn't have asked to have this

A. we really do

C. this little check in this little

A. we know that your time is very valuable

C. little pow-pow

B. oh that's

A. pow-wow

C. if we didn't think you'd be equally as excited

B. that's okay

C. about this idea this possibility

A. Opportunity

C. yes opportunity really

A. And the advances in technology are just

C. my daughter is a huge fan of yours

A. incredible. oh mine too mine too

C. I just had to say. and my Son

A. The album with the with the upside-down ice cream cone on the cover

B. Yeah

A. I thought the music was incredibly Funky

C. my Son is, I mean, You Are. He has your pictures all over his walls. not to make you uncomfortable or or. he's fifteen so not far off your age but anyway it's really quite extraordinary the sheer quantity of images. From now but also all through your career. The whole thing. And he spends so much time in there, so much time. I mean the mind boggles really. Some days I go up there to bring him his lunch or one of the little yoghurt pots he likes and I open the door and there he is just staring

A. ha!

C. he likes your music too of course but you know how teenage boys are

A. ha disgusting ha

C. and you're very. this is okay to say isn't it

A. I think it is. I think it's okay

C. you're beautiful

A. beautiful

C. really

A. near perfect

(They wait.)

B. thank you

C. Eighty-seven.

B. sorry?

C. That's how many pictures he has. My son. I counted once. Took forever.

oh boy he'll kill me for mentioning the yoghurt pots

D. She has a dance rehearsal in four minutes.

A. yes!

B. I'm sorry

D. So if you could

C. yes. yes.

/ let me just get. this. set. up.

A. you must have a lot of dance rehearsals

B. I guess

A. all that Funky dancing

C. Okay so.

Here's what we're proposing. And this is just a prototype but

A. Take a look.

B. it's me

A. / no

C. yes

A. well yes but not precisely

C. we scanned you. every inch. so she's an exact replica. every single part of her body, her facial expressions, the way she moves is basically. it's completely the same. but also, not better exactly but

A. no

C. she doesn't need to eat

A. not 'better' but

C. or sleep

A. think of the opportunity. from a purely financial standpoint. because as it stands you're a non-scalable resource

C. if we send her out on the road you can be filling two three five stadiums at once. more. and you wouldn't even need to be there

B. sorry?

C. you could do whatever you want. you could go catch a movie with a small group of friends

A. or sleep

C. yeah you could sleep till any time of the day. eat what you like. go shopping

A. she can dance too

B. I can dance

C. but she can do it for you

B. but I like dancing

A. oh sure.

but you know

C. she doesn't even sweat

A. she's physically incapable of sweating

B. my fans wouldn't like it

A. They like you very much

B. She's not me

C. They wouldn't be able to tell

B. they would

C. There are zero physical differences

B. she's not real

A. sure.

but what is real, really?

B. she's not a person

A. well

B. That's not a person

C. look at her

I feel like I could reach out and touch her

B. I

C. the thing is, and excuse me for saying this, but you will soon be in your twenties

A. we're so sorry

C. and your fanbase isn't aging. so there really are so many opportunities we could explore

A. She has your voice too

C. yes, she is you now but if we wanted, if everyone wanted, she could be you, say, a year ago

A. she experiences no pain. no physical or emotional distress

C. or two years. or longer.

A. did you know that in Korea they have whole bands. whole bands of girls who don't even exist. incredible.

C. like a preserved memory of you

A. there's so much money to be made in the teenage market

C. never changing

A. your fans will love her

C. fourteen forever

A. isn't that the dream

C. everyone could make so much money

B. the guys at the label. they want me to do this?

D. they think it's an option

*(**B** looks at the virtual version of herself.)*

C. We could make her smaller. If you wanted

B. what did you just say to me?

A. I think what we're saying is that if you wanted there could be

C. there could be tweaks

A. yeah. tweaks

D. tweaks are an option

C. little tweaks

nose perhaps

A. it's an option

B. oh

okay

C. like if you wanted she could be per–

Shoplifting – Before Now

(**B** *steals a lipstick.)*

A. Put that back.

B. Are you talking to me?

A. In your pocket. I saw you. Put it back

B. There's nothing

A. I'll tell

you can't do that. i'll fetch a cashier

B. You should take one

You know you can just do it, right?

This is your colour

Take one
What are they going to do?

Just take one.

Incel – Now

(**A** *packs his bag.* **B** *watches.*)

A. they don't check bags on Thursdays. or they do but it's not, it's Mr Cooper who does it and he doesn't even, it's just for show really, and sometimes he makes like a joke out of it you know or he like takes your snacks like your lunch or whatever, and it's a joke like this, like he does this voice you know? like the cookie monster? like Me WaNt ChIpStIcKs or like like **mE WaNt YoUr GrAnDmA's Oa-OaTmEaL cHoCoLaTe TrAyBaKe WiTh ThE LiTtLe PiEcEs Of PoPpInG cAnDy RoOaAARgHHHH**

um.

it's actually, it's actually pretty funny when he does it, or it's not but yeah. and anyway my Grandma's traybake slaps so, and Mr Cooper knows my dad actually, so like we're cool, like I'm pretty tight with Mr Cooper.

or I thought even that I could tell him that the bag inside, you know the bag with the Thing in it, that it's actually stuff that I'm bringing for my little sister, like stuff for when she's on her, like a box of of of of

B. tampons?

A. so obviously he won't look inside that to find out that it isn't, and then I'm inside the building then. so probably fifth period is when I'll ask to go to the bathroom because I have this stuff that I want to wear, balaclava, long coat, sunglasses, it's kind of part of the Message. and I was thinking I'd go to the one in the art block actually because it's furthest from the street, and also all the doors down there have that window so you can see inside, so even if they lock the doors I can just shoot through and reach down. it's really very, it's really very poorly designed. and it's all about speed then essentially because I'll have to keep reloading, and I only have so

many rounds too, you know? so like it's gonna be about being kind of selective of which females
also I know you have art fifth period right?

cool so this is just your warning for that. I thought it might be nice to give you a heads up. och just a like a wee, a wee spoiler alert that you might wanna lock yourself in a cupboard or whatever

B. yeah thanks

A. but don't film anything though. I don't want that.
So what I'm thinking is I'll hit 5c, b, d, e, then if I make it past that

B. um

A. I can go round. they have ballet

B. it's

A. yeah?

B. nothing.

A. yeah?

Are you scared? cos. like. you know you don't need to be scared

B. I know

A. I'll protect you

B. yeah

A. I'm not a pussy

B. I know

I know that

A. hey
you know that they aren't real, right?

B. what?

A. they aren't real. like. if you reached out, your hand would go right through them

B. that's not

A. you're real though. aren't you. I can tell.

aren't you?

B. the new girl is in 5e and she absolutely loves herself

A. okay nice. maybe I'll go there first then

Soldiers Three

(All the girls perform a synchronised TikTok-style dance, each wearing clothes from a different era. Perhaps they're wearing sunglasses.)

(Something like "Girls To The Front" by Diet Punk. Supremely confident in their sexuality and all their weird, sticky, aggressiveness.)*

(Pure power.)

---

* A licence to produce *We Could All Be Perfect* does not include a performance licence for "Girls to the Front". The publisher and author suggest that the licensee contact PRS to ascertain the music publisher and contact such music publisher to license or acquire permission for performance of the song. If a licence or permission is unattainable for "Girls to the Front", the licensee may not use the song in *We Could All Be Perfect* but should create an original composition in a similar style or use a similar song in the public domain. For further information, please see the Music and Third-Party Materials Use Note on page iii.

Gift – Now

*(**B** is holding a gift.)*

A. Well?

B. Oh!
Oh it's
You've got me

you've

A. It's

B. Yeah!

A. With little ice cream cones on it because

B. Right

A. They're your favourite

B. Were

A. And you're always

B. Were / my favourite

A. always wearing things with little ice cream cones printed on them so

B. Well

A. That's you

You're welcome

B. Thanks sorry thanks

They're not anymore

A. Sorry?

B. I don't anymore though

A. Don't you like it?

B. No yeah I'm just saying that I don't actually wear things with

A. Yes you do, they're your favourite

B. They're not

A. They are

B. They're not though

A. You wear them all the time. Literally

B. I don't though

A. Constantly. Little ice cream cones

B. You're wrong though

A. Incessant

B. Right well I actually despise them now.

A. So what do you like now then?

B. Lemon wedges

Girl – Before Now

A. the elders sent me

B. Again?
This is the third time since harvest.

A. yes

B. Closer to the fire so I can see you.

Take that off.

A. no

B. Take it off.

A. no

B. Do you want me to do what I did last time?

Closer. Look at me.

A. the fire's hot

B. What are you?

A. I am a girl.

B. No. What are you?

A. I am a girl.

B. What are you?

B. I am a girl.

B. Listen to me. Listen. You are a boy. You're my boy

A. no

B. you're my boy

A. No

B. Tell me what you are.

A. Girl.

B. You know what girls get. Do you want that?

What are you?

A. I am a girl.

B. stop it. I love you. stop it

Supermarket Five – Now

(Outside the supermarket.)

*(***SECRET** *lies on the floor at* **LESSONS'** *feet.)*

LESSONS. Open the door!

OPEN THE DOOR

Get up
Come on get up
Can you get up?
please

We have to keep going

SHE'S LITERALLY FREEZING
JUST OPEN

I'LL HAVE SEX WITH YOU IF YOU OPEN THE DOOR IS THAT WHAT YOU WANT?

IF YOU JUST LET HER IN

IF YOU JUST LET ME IN

please

I'M GOING TO FUCKING KILL YOU

I'M GOING TO FUCKING KILL YOU

OPEN

6

Haircut – Now

A. All of it

B. you want me to

A. Literally all of it.

B. okay so. okay so. so is it like are we talking like a nice pixie like a

A. You're not listening to me.

B. I'm not sure I'm fully understanding babe

A. I want you to shave it all off

B. You don't want that

A. Yes I do.

B. You don't want that

A. I'm telling you.

B. no you think you do but you don't babes because you've got lovely haven't you got lovely

A. I know what I want.

B. you've got lovely long

A. Shave it all off.

B. I'm not going to do that am I

A. You have to.

B. I wouldn't do that to you would I

A. I'm asking

B. you would be needing your parent's permission though. I would be needing a parent here present.

A. Why?

B. What about a fringe? a fringe can solve all sorts of

A. no thank you

B. lovely fringe

A. no

B. nice fringe. little fringe. butterfly fringe

A. stop saying fringe

B. Are you okay my love?

A. Yes.

B. Is this a cry for help

A. no I just

B. I'm hearing a cry for help

A. It's not a cry for help

B. Do you want to have a little lie down

A. I'm fine

B. let's tip the chair back so we can have a lie down

A. It's a haircut

B. I couldn't let you do that to yourself could I

A. give me the razor

B. No

A. I'll do it anyway.

B. no. no. you mustn't

A. I'm going to. It's my body, it's my

Kiss – Now

(Light overhead.)

A. She wanted everyone to watch.

B. No

A. She did she did. She goes "if you don't do it now in front of everyone. if you don't kiss him now then you're frigid"

B. Piss off no

*(**B** waves his arms in the air.)*

A. "and you can't take a joke". And our kid just stands there. Gawping. Mouth hanging open like some like some

*(**B** waves his arms in the air.)*

B. Yeah?

A. like some broken cd case and doesn't do nothing

B. Am gonna kill her

A. Or say nothing or

*(**B** waves his arms in the air.)*

B. Am gonna pull his teeth out

A. Sorry. Why do you keep doing that?

B. What?

*(**B** waves his arms in the air.)*

A. That. Waving your arms around like you're

B. Ah

A. tryna land a plane or

B. right

A. in peril at sea

Why –

B. Wait
Don't move

(They both stay completely still.)

(The light goes off. Complete darkness.)

A. Oh

B. Security light. S'buggered. Mum's been on to the council. Doesn't see anything here, but here

*(**B** waves his arms. The light comes back on.)*

A. huh

B. did you, like
did you want to?

A. Want to?

B. kiss him

A. No

B. if they weren't watching

A. am not scared

*(**A** waves her hands in the air.)*

B. Do you like him?

A. I properly hate him now

B. I properly hate him now too

A. Thanks

B. Have you kissed before?

A. Yeah loads of people

B. oh

A. You?

B. no nobody

A. no yeah me neither actually

(They both wave their hands.)

Do you want to?

B. Like generally?

A. Yeah generally. or. or now

with me

you could kiss me

you don't have

B. yeah

A. shit really?

B. if you still want to

A. yeah. yes. yes. yeah.

okay

B. yeah

A. I've completely forgotten what I normally do with my hands now

B. same

A. Should we go somewhere else or?

B. erm

keep still

(The light goes off.)

A. Slow

(They kiss.)

*(***B*** waves his arms and the light comes back on.)*

Yeah.

Send Nudes – Now

A. And?

B. right

A. Yeah?

B. yeah um
um

they aren't exactly what I

A. No? no

B. yeah

A. In a good way?

B. in a yeah no in an unexpected way. like. woooooooo

A. okay?

B. it's just um okay it's just you know with us and with everything that's been happening and we're good yeah like we've been messaging like talking and that and so I thought yeah we're at that level we're probably definitely at that level where maybe (and this is why I messaged you) maybe you would be up for sending
some

nudes

A. Yep.

B. yep

and these are

A. Nudes

B. right, but you've

A. I've drawn them. Yep.

B. Nice
Nice.

It's just I thought they might be you know like like like like photos or

A. Oh!

B. I mean it's probably my

I probably should have been more specific about what I

A. No

B. It's cool that they're like retro you know like analogue like analogue nudes

A. yeah wind-up nudes yeah

B. and the way you put them in my planner without actually at all telling me you were gonna do that so they'd just fall out onto my desk in the middle of DT like whaaaaaaaa!

A. Sexy surprise!

B. Mhmm mhmm you got me!
but it wasn't in an exact sense

A. Gotcha

B. what I was

A. Yeah no definitely I did actually take some photos some explicit

B. **Wow! Amazing!**

A. Yeah but then I thought this way was actually way better.

B. okay?

A. Because then you'd get more of a sense of of of

B. right

A. And then once I started drawing it was like this this heat came over me like this primal, ancient
Because there are certain things that a photo can't show, you know? So then eventually I came to thinking that this way was more effective really because then I could just show you *everything*. All the stuff that people *can't* see.

B. they're quite
quite quite quite quite

A. Aggressive?

B. ***Terrifying***. Yes. *Scary* and

A. Yeah feral. That surprised me too. Exciting.

(They look at the drawings.)

B. What's this?

A. That's this bit. It's one of my favourite bits.

B. And this one is? Those are uh

A. Oh yeah Snakes

B. Growing from your

A. Head. Yep.

B. right

A. Aren’t I beauti

Supermarket Six – Now

(Outside the supermarket. The new girl is **B** *from* **INCEL.***)*

*(***SECRET** *is still in a bad way.)*

INCEL. is she okay?

are you okay?

LESSONS. it's just us right now. but there are more coming

INCEL. how long have you been out here? how long have you been waiting?

LESSONS. we aren't waiting anymore

INCEL. what then?

LESSONS. getting ready

War – Now

(**A** *steps up to a podium.*)

A. Thank you all for inviting me to speak to you today.

This is an extraordinary opportunity I have to speak to some of the most powerful people in the world, people who are able to make immediate change. So many of you here in one room. Wow. And to think it was you who were asking me for selfies before I came up here.

Sorry, can you hear me alright?

This isn't my first language so I'm sorry if I do not speak it perfectly at first. I'm learning. I'm sure you will get the gist.

Shall I begin?

Usually I start these speeches with a a a shocking statistic perhaps. A quantification of the time left on the clock to make change. A list of rising things; temperature, sea-levels.
It's boring, yes?
Repetitive? Um, performance maybe? You give your time and do your bit, as you say, by listening with a look on your face like this while I get angry and say a lot of numbers. It's alright, you can laugh.
You know what, I think today I will do things a little differently. So, for the sake of time, let's say I've given those facts and you, you've done those faces.

Is my English okay?

I have to admit, I do not like your language so much as mine. It is more, what is it, brutal. Anyway

I have given speeches like this quite a few times before. I should be in school instead, many of you would say rather than bossing you around and you're right, I should. I think this will be my last speech like this actually. This is the last one. I'm sorry. We will have to find another way to get the selfies.

So, you're killing us.

We've told you this. You are choosing to do nothing and as direct result of that choice many millions of people will die. It won't be tomorrow but it will happen. Perhaps you will kill my daughter, or my daughter's son, or his. If you do not make the necessary changes in the next year then the situation is irreversible. This will definitely happen. You will have definitely killed people. In fact, specifically your own children's children.

Sorry, can you see me alright behind this?

It comes to me that we are in a kind of slow war. You are killing so slowly with your multi-million-dollar businesses and your pandering for votes that maybe you don't even realise you're doing it. Except I've told you. We keep telling you. I have been angry with you, I have reasoned with you, I have asked nicely. So, what is it? You don't care? You're stupid? You're slow?

Don't worry, I don't think it's that. I think maybe you don't understand my language. I keep forgetting. I shouldn't expect you to learn to speak it. We are in your country after all.

It's very useful for you that it is not in our nature as young people, specifically young women, to be violent. I don't believe in it. It's cruel, it isn't it's not erm helpful. I don't like violence. I am just a child. I don't want to be here. But you love that I am a child. You say this girl, she gives me hope. One day, one day she will make everything better. And you don't have to do anything. So that's why this will be my final speech.

And today is the day that we will all save the world.

Are you getting all this? Can you see me alright? I am quite small. If I stood on a box perhaps.

I think I am getting better at your language. Do you agree? Yes?

That's good, that's nice. It makes me a little sad to speak it, I have to say. I do not believe in your slow war. Your endless violation of a planet that does not belong to you.

I do not believe in using violence as a tool. I don't.

But you do.

If you do not learn my language, eventually I will speak yours.

You can see me? Okay. Good

Are you ready?

Can we lock the doors now please?

Could you stop that woman?

Thank you so much.

I have some demands.

7

The Perfectionists – Soon

(Inside the supermarket.)

*(***SECRET, LESSONS*** and ***INCEL*** and joined by the girls from ***FORK*** and ***WAR****.)*

*(***WAR*** sits a little apart.)*

(At least one of them is eating from a tin.)

LESSONS. Are we the first? I think we could be the first.

SECRET. I hope we are

LESSONS. I think we actually might be. We're the first to see exactly how everything needs changing. And we can actually do it now. We're the first to finally realise just how everything should be

FORK. We're going to fix everything

INCEL. everyone always thought that

SECRET. It's different now.

LESSONS. It's actually kind of cruel that before we were the only people who could see what needed to be done and the only ones who never had the power to actually make anything happen

INCEL. it was literally always that

FORK. That's not true.

SECRET. Which?

FORK. We did have the power.

LESSONS. Not actually

FORK. Malala Yousafzai. Dora Thewlis. Barbara Johns. X Gonzalez. Joan of fucking Arc

LESSONS. Not in like a legislative

SECRET. A lot of them suffered.

FORK. oh my god put ketchup on the lentils it's amazing

SECRET. Do you think we have to suffer?

LESSONS. Martyrs

FORK. What teenage girl didn't suffer?

INCEL. it's not real. it's just a feeling

it was like this for everyone. everyone had this moment of clarity when they were our age. this period of time when they thought could see everything with absolute clarity. see all the bad in the world and all the ways to make it better. and then they just lost it. whoompf. soon as they were old enough to actually change anything

FORK. I never had a feeling that wasn't real.

SECRET. We could be wrong.

LESSONS. Can you chew less loudly please. I can literally hear you masticating.

WAR. We're not wrong.

SECRET. No. I know. We're not wrong

(The girls all gather round Secret's dying phone. The last one. Suddenly –.)

SECRET. One / percent!

FORK. One / percent!

LESSONS. Oh /my god

INCEL. Oh/ my oh my

LESSONS. Balance it on the beans

FORK. Quick. Last one

(They huddle together.)

SECRET. Ready?

(They take a group selfie with the phone. It should be whatever the actors feel like on the night, so long as it isn't actively pretty.)

*(**SECRET** checks the phone.)*

Dead!

(They all cheer.)

(A moment of joy. Laughter.)

LESSONS. Okay but can we all just agree this whole thing has been really fucking embarrassing?

FORK. Okay so. Okay so. Why don't we start with, what are the rules?

LESSONS. No rules.

SECRET. There have to be rules.

LESSONS. Rules got us into this mess.

FORK. What's the idea then?

LESSONS. A place for just us

FORK. No adults.

LESSONS. Adults got us into this mess

SECRET. But I like adults

LESSONS. No boys

FORK. Noooo. I love boys

LESSONS. Just for now at least. Just for the beginning while we work everything out. We've got everything we need to survive here and its safe so no one can get us. No one can d-word.

We'll make new stuff. And when it's ready we can give it to everyone else.

INCEL. What happens when we grow up?

SECRET. We won't.

LESSONS. It's against the rules.
And we should vote. On everything.

SECRET. I've always wanted to do that

FORK. Like a state?

LESSONS. Kind of.

SECRET. A republic. Where everyone's just teenage g

FORK. They proved that the best way to solve global poverty and reverse climate change is to educate girls. When I grow up, in the new world, I'll have only daughters.

INCEL. Who's 'they'

LESSONS. What are you going to do? Kill your sons?

FORK. I. No

SECRET. That's awful

LESSONS. How would that even work?

FORK. I haven't considered logistics

INCEL. I won't have any children. I will have an ethical company and do a job I would be happy to do even if I wasn't being paid. I will take a lover from time to time. I'll wear tailored suits and heels with my hair long so people will know I'm approachable

LESSONS. Do you know the carbon footprint of having a child?

FORK. I know I shouldn't want them. I try to stop myself but I do.

INCEL. I'll have two dogs. Dalmatians.

SECRET. Nothing you want can ever be bad

LESSONS. Alright we'll round up all the girls then. The girls already born without homes or bad ones or. And teach them.

INCEL. How?

LESSONS. I don't know. It's an idea. It's the idea that matters. Not the how.

FORK. Whenever you're ready.

*(**INCEL** screams.)*

*(After a second **WAR** joins in.)*

(They stop.)

(They look up.)

INCEL. Do you think they heard us?

FORK. You have to make them think it's their idea. The adults. You have to get inside their heads.

Like, my mum is magic. She did this amazing thing, right?

It's like this one time all I ate for a month was lemons. I didn't put anything in my mouth but perfect yellow lemons and I got it into my head that that was all I needed to survive. But then that's a lot of sugar and I lost a lot of weight you know. My ribs poked out. You could see each one like the bottom of shipwreck. And eventually between my fingers started wrinkling and my tongue turned white and my hair all smelled like lemon which you would think would be a nice thing but actually it was more like that rotten smell. You know the one I mean? Like a dead thing. But still I was eating lemons, until one day my mum was baking this cake. And she told me she didn't have nothing to put in it. It was a birthday cake I remember and she was sad that the cake would be plain. So I gave her some of my lemons to be baked into it. She made it seem like I was helping her but actually she was helping me. Both. The same. Because then it happened I could eat the cake too because somehow it was my idea and also somehow it was a part of me.

LESSONS. Does anyone else want cake now?

(They've made a cake. At least one girl eats it.)

(At least one girl is drawing.)

(Someone is piercing someone else's ear with an ice cube and a needle. The girl being pierced can say the word "ow" as many times as she likes.)

*(***SECRET*** and ***INCEL*** can talk over each other at times.)*

SECRET. Okay, what if it's what if it's this. Just start from the beginning but better. What if it's that we just say like no cars this time round. No power stations or

INCEL. I sometimes feel that if I just had a different nose everything would be sorted. I know you're not supposed to think that but it's true. If I could just fix my nose then I could deal with all the everything of the world.

SECRET. Or everyone gets like a like a like an allocation of energy.

INCEL. If my nose were thinner and my eyebrows straighter and I had some different bone structure then people would want to be around me more.

SECRET. A certain size your carbon footprint can be. And you can choose how you use it but everyone gets their fair share

INCEL. I think I take up too much space. I don't know at all what to do with my hands. I know I should stand up straighter. I practice but then I see myself in the background of a photo. I see the shape of the curve of my neck my shoulders and I want to die.

SECRET. No oil companies. No private jets. No billionaires.

INCEL. If I could stand up straight and fix my nose I think. It's not the same for other people. I think they should be however they are and they're beautiful and I can see that. But me specifically I should be better than I am.

FORK. It's not realistic

LESSONS. Are we being realistic this time?

INCEL. I really think we could be perfect. Don't you? If we all just tried little harder.

SECRET. If we changed things.

INCEL. I think if we tried we could all be perfect.

(A lemon drops from the ceiling.)

(They all stop and look at it.)

FORK. Can everyone else see that?

SECRET. I feel funny

FORK. It's the food.

SECRET. Does anyone else feel funny?

INCEL. When are we?

SECRET. I feel like I might throw up or

LESSONS. You went a long time without eating

SECRET. I feel itchy.

INCEL. It's almost certainly your period.

LESSONS. Don't say that.

INCEL. What? It's normally my period.

LESSONS. You can't say that

SECRET. I feel like my fingers are growing.

WAR. I've had that

FORK. When?

WAR. I used to have that

SECRET. Are they?
Can you see?

LESSONS. Show me

SECRET. I have a feeling in my
It's just a thought but
Like I don't know this is silly this is bleugh but
okay um

I'm starting to get the feeling that I'm probably the most powerful thing in existence?
Do you know what I mean?
Like pure potential.
Like I have this sense that um I could probably swallow oceans actually. Just, you know, as an example.

Like, I'm pretty confident could consume the world and walk.
And there's this itching between my shoulder blades that kind of feels like wings.

I could paint myself on a stained-glass windows,
couldn't you?

Ha!

God what am I going to be?
I'm on the starting line, aren't you?

Can you feel that we're all just on the starting line?

Milton Keynes UK
Ingram Content Group UK Ltd.
UKHW022053130923
428647UK00002B/3

9 780573 000393